Tarot & Nakshatras 2

Copyright

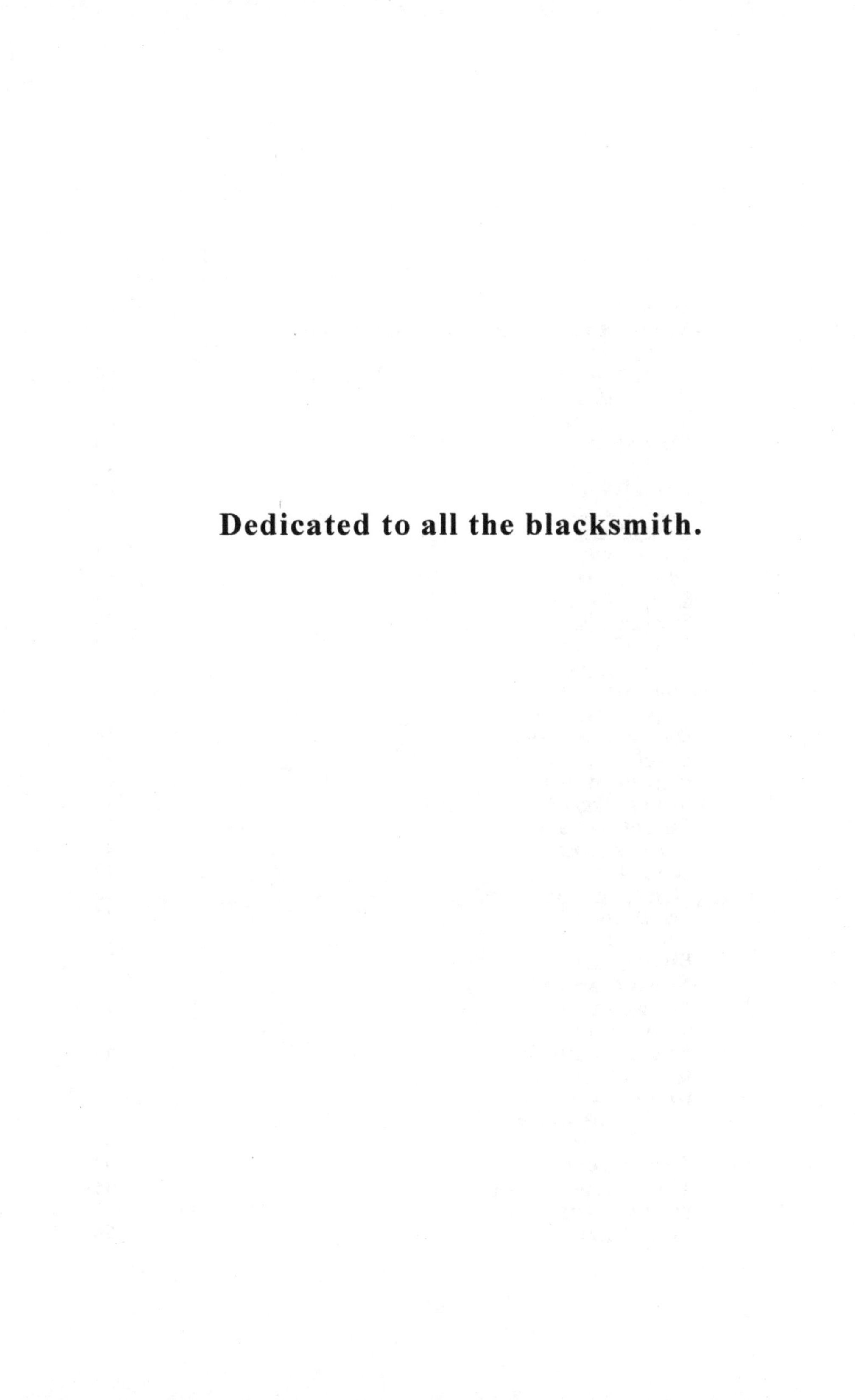

Dedicated to all the blacksmith.

Contents

Foreword

After the blacksmith beheaded the serpent in its last encounter. It caught the attention of entire tribe of the serpents including the kings and queens. The whole tribe was so jealous and envious of the blacksmith that they wanted to settle a score with him. In the moment of jealousy and hate they forgot the dharma of their profession and turned rogue. All rogue serpents started spitting venom everywhere without realising the consequences it had on the masses. It was a spectacle of sheer abuse of power and position. The blacksmith knew he can't handle the whole tribe on his own, so he pulled another move up his sleeve. He stroke his hammer so hard on the anvil that the sound echoed through the woods. All the nearby blacksmith heard the sound and they knew it was a war cry at once. All of them together stroke their hammers on the anvil and slowly it became a rhythm. All the rogue serpents were taken aback by the rhythm and they knew there is not much that can be done. In this book you will know how to connect different dots to make a rhythm!

Beginner's guide: How to read this book

This book is a sequel to Tarot & Nakshatras. All those readers who have already read the previous book may skip this section.

A reader must be aware of Tarot cards specifically Rider-Waite Tarot deck and a fair understanding of astrological houses as well as nakshatras.

This book gives a different perspective on the archetype of Rider-Waite Tarot deck. It shows the uncanny resemblance of nakshatras working day in day out with all of our lives as well as tries to bridge the gap among faiths, after all we are not so different, maybe a little!

There are twelve zodiac signs namely:

Aries, Taurus, Gemini, Cancer, Leo, Virgo, Libra, Scorpio, Sagittarius, Capricorn, Aquarius, Pisces.

And there are twelve houses in astrology each with a significance:

1st house: self, ascendant, appearance, vigour, innate nature etc.

2nd house: speech (vocal cords), wealth, values, food etc.

3rd house: brothers, sisters, communication, short journey, neighbour etc.

4th house: mother, relatives, land and houses, happiness etc.

5th house: knowledge, primary learning, children, creativity, royalty etc.

6th house: debts, known enemies, maternal uncle, obstacles etc.

7th house: spouse/partner, trading partnership, death /transformation etc.

8th house: longevity, hidden enemies, occult, inheritance etc.

9th house: fortunes, religion, higher learning, long distance travel, father/father figure etc.

10th house: profession(livelihood), royalty, fame etc.

11th house: income, gains, pets, prosperity etc.

12th house: expenses, emancipation, isolation etc.

Nakshatra are the lunar mansions used in Vedic astrology. It is the elliptical path ('Naks' -sky, 'Shetra' -area/map) of the moon through the stars. Moon cycle is of 27.3 days; the time it takes to travel through its orbit. Considering equal divisions of 27 lunar mansions of the 360^0 zodiac, each nakshatra spans out over 13.33^0 which are further divided into four padas (legs signified as Dharma, Artha, Kama and Moksha).

The **27 Nakshtaras** (lunar constellation) are; **Ashwini, Bharani, Krittika, Rohini, Mrigasira, Ardra, Punarvasu, Pushya, Ashlesha, Magha, Purva Phalguni, Uttara Phalguni, Hasta, Chitra, Swati, Vishakha, Anuradha, Jyestha, Mula, Purva Asadha, Uttara Asadha, Shravana, Dhanistha, Satabhishaj, Purva Bhadrapada, Uttara Bhadrapada, Revati.**

The 27 nakshatras and their themes are associated with Hindu mythological stories which repeat itself overtime. If an event repeat itself once or twice it's a coincidence (or an outlier) but when it happens over and over again then it becomes eternal. Themes of nakshatras are not only applicable to mortals but even to Devas (Angels) and Asuras (Demons). To delve into the themes of nakshatra, it would require a series of book of its own which is beyond the scope of this book. Inquisitive readers are advised to do their own research on Nakshatras.

A brief note on Rider-Waite Tarot deck: It was created by Arthur Edward Waite and Pamela Colman Smith. In this book we will use the word 'creator' to refer both of them.

Rider-Waite Tarot deck consist of 78 cards out of which there are 22 major arcana and 4 suits of minor arcana consisting of 14 cards each. Minor arcana suits are

Wands (Fire element/Aries, Leo, Sagittarius/Action),

Cups (Water element/Cancer, Scorpio, Pisces/ Emotions),

Pentacles (Earth element/Taurus, Virgo, Capricorn/ Anything tangible),

Swords (Air element/ Gemini, Libra, Aquarius/ Communication).

This book delves into the themes of 56 minor arcana cards (4 suits of 14 cards each) for better understanding.

Suit of Cups

King of Cups

Symbols	Possibilities/ Significance
Golden fish	connection with Egypt fish goddess Hatmehyt/ a family heirloom.
Red ship	danger/ship caught in turbulence.

A big fish	whale/ shark/ heavy turbulence in sea that exposes such a big fish.
A cup or chalice	water/emotions.
Scepter	king or royal figure.
Person sitting on elevated platform	despite turbulence the platform is dry/one who controls the sea/ one who created the turbulence and thus unaffected by it.

Theme : The card is a depiction of Moses during the exodus of Israelites from Egypt. Moses uses his staff to part the red sea(depicted by the red ships in the image) so that the Israelites can cross on dry ground but the sea closes down on the pursuing Egyptians.

Zodiac sign	Pisces.
Nakshatra	Uttara Bhadrapada(Deity - Ahir Budhnya; water dragon)

Tarot meaning	Leading people, magical powers, someone who works for the community, powerful person to be reckoned with, a healer, convincing speaker, someone who will help you in your goals, hermits, prophets, Venus in Uttara Bhadrapada and themes of Uttara Bhadrapada nakshatra.
Overall vibe	positive or affirmative.

Queen of Cups

Symbols	**Possibilities/ Significance**
Flowing water	river/lake/sea.
Pebbles at the bottom of the female figure	shore of the lake/river.
Woman with a crown	queen/royal figure.
A big chalice with a symbol of cross on top and two angels like figure standing on either side	family heirloom/big chalice/religious artefact/ connection with jewish culture.
Two children on top of the chair	keeping an eye on the artefact(chalice).

One child with waves behind and fish in hand at the side of the chair	child birth/connection of child with water or fish/ fisherman's child.

Theme : The card is a depiction of Pharaoh's daughter who rescued baby Moses from the banks of river Nile. Jews were under slavery during the Exodus. When the Pharaoh of Egypt ordered to kill all the male children of Israelites due to the threat of rebellion from their growing population. Moses' biological mother was Jochebed. She feared for the life of the baby so she put Moses in a reed basket (reference to the big chalice in the image) and put it among the reeds along the bank of Nile. Moses elder sister Miriam stood at a distance to see what would happen to the child(reference to the kids on top of the chair in the image).

Pharaoh's daughter went down to river Nile to bathe and the saw the kid in the basket. Pharaoh's daughter asked one of her servants to take the baby and nurse him, in return she will pay for her services. The name Moses was given by Pharaoh's daughter herself which means " I drew him out of the water".

Keywords : Adopting someone's child and raising them as your own, sea, fish.

Zodiac sign	Pisces.
Nakshatra	Revati.
Tarot	caregiver, foster parenting,
meaning	compassionate, work with children, born
Overall	positive or affirmative.

Knight of Cups

Symbols	**Possibilities/ Significance**
Mountains in background and river flowing	Nile river and its surrounding / any river
A knight holding a cup	offering something/ leading
Red fish symbol on armour	connected to Nile/Red sea during Exodus from Egypt
Horse head is down and not galloping	horse is not willing to move forward/ danger ahead/horse is scared of the water

Theme: The card is a depiction of Nashon. Nashon was a tribal leader of Judahites during Exodus. He was an Israelite as well as Judahite. Nashon's sister Elisheba married Aaron(elder brother of Moses). Nashon was appointed by Moses as prince and military commander of the tribe of Judah and one of the tribes of Israel. During Exodus, when Israelites reached the red sea, it did not part automatically. But as soon as Nashon entered the water it started to part particularly when he was upto his nose in the water(reference to the cup at the level of nose in the above image). As per legends this is the origin of his name Nashol that is "stormy sea waves".

Keywords : Leader, chief of the tribe.

Zodiac sign Scorpio.

Nakshatra	Jyestha.
Tarot	chief of the tribe, one who takes
meaning	initiative, intrinsic motivation and themes
Overall	positive or affirmative.

Page of Cups

Symbols	**Possibilities/ Significance**
Waves of water in the background	river shore.
Young man holding a chalice with a fish in it.	fisherman/caught a fish/a catch.
Lotus on clothes	Nile river reference/royal family/noble birth.

Theme: The card is a depiction of young Moses being brought up in Egypt and donning the dress of royal family. He was adopted by the Pharaoh's daughter.

Despite Moses being a jewish he got into the good graces of royal family where all other Hebrews were slaves during the Exodus. He grew up as a child with comforts. The image shows the young man is contented and happy.

Keywords: Away from home, contented with whatever available, born in someplace but raised somewhere else, being fortunate.

Zodiac sign	Cancer.
Nakshatra	Pushya.
Tarot	contented with little, fortunate, connected
meaning	to fisheries, a fine catch and themes of
Overall	positive or affirmative.

Ace of Cups

Symbols	Possibilities/ Significance
Cup/chalice	for pouring water.
Letter W or M in inverted	reference to someone's initials such as Moses or Miriam.
White dove	messengers of peace or love.
A coin with plus symbol brought by the dove	symbol could represent Jerusalem/coin/birds can carry small stones or coins.

Cup is overflowing with five streams	abundance.
Hand from the cloud	sign from God/divine intervention.
Lotus at the bottom of the image	due to water or abundance from the cup lotus is blossoming/ creation/ connection to Nile river/ Egypt connection.

Theme: The card is a depiction of Miriam's well(reference to cup in the above image). Miriam was older sister of Moses and Aaron. She was also an important person during the Exodus of Israelites from Egypt. Moses led the men of Egypt and taught them Torah and Miriam led the women and did the same. As per legend Aron was gifted clouds of glory, Moses was given manna and Miriam was given the well by the God. Miriam's well nourished all the jews during that time. It is said that after Miriam's death the well dried up. It is also a popular practice in Jewish culture to drink from the cup as a homage to Miriam.

Keywords : Nourishment, knowledge of divinity.

Zodiac sign	Cancer.
Nakshatra	Pushya.
Tarot meaning Overall	nourishment, knowledge of divinity, new beginnings, caregiver and themes of positive or affirmative.

Two of Cups

Symbols	Possibilities/ Significance
Woman with red shoes	a high priestess/someone from aristocrat background/connection with priest/connection with power.
Woman wearing a wreath on head	wreath of olive/wreath is donned during wedding.
Man in normal attire	average family or background.

Man wearing a wreath of flower	wreath of roses/wreath of unknown flower/for wedding purpose.
Caduceus symbol	a symbol for alchemy.
A winged lion on top of Caduceus	connection with Egypt/ red faced colour shows power
Woman offering cup with both hands	emotional connection/ complete devotion/ desire.
Man is stopping the cup offered to him with his right hand	refusing/reluctant.
Symbol of clover on clothes of man	good luck/connection with marriage and rituals in ancient Egypt.

Theme: The card is a depiction of marriage of Joseph and Asenath (daughter of a priest) also the wife of Potiphar(ambiguity exists whether wife or daughter).

Jospeh was sold into slavery by his own brothers. He ended up in Egypt and became the servant of Potiphar.

Potiphar's adulterous wife tried to seduce Joseph, which he refused. After this Potiphar's wife accused Joseph of rape and as a result Joseph was put into prison.

Joseph had the ability to interpret dreams since his childhood. When Pharaoh of the Egypt had a dream which no one could interpret, he asked Joseph to interpret it. Pharaoh's dream was interpreted as seven years of abundance followed by seven years of famine. Pharaoh was impressed by Joseph's intelligence and he employed him to re-organise grain supplies of Egypt. Pharaoh made sure Joseph marries a high born woman to get the respect he deserves.

Overall theme shows that Joseph used his intelligence to turn his miserable condition (in prison) into a situation of hope and power, a sheer example of "true alchemy".

Zodiac sign Cancer.

Nakshatra	Ashlesha.
Tarot	poisonous relationships, alchemist,
meaning	cunning, achieving power and themes of
Overall	neutral.

Three of Cups

<u>**Symbols**</u>	<u>**Possibilities/ Significance**</u>
Three women each holding a chalice	a crowd/gathering/ celebration.
Pumpkin at the bottom and lots of fruits in the background	abundance/farmers/ agricultural community.

Theme: The card is a depiction of the dance 'Horah' of Jews. It is danced during celebration or jewish wedding. Above card shows small groups as represented by three people.

Zodiac sign	Pisces.
Nakshatra	Uttara Bhadrapada.
Tarot meaning	celebration, community gathering, wedding, season of good harvest and
Overall	positive or affirmative.

Four of Cups

<u>Symbols</u>	**<u>Possibilities/ Significance</u>**
Man sitting under tree cross legged and arms crossed	posture is defensive/ reluctant/stubborn.
Three cups in front of him	not satisfied with the cups
One cup is offered from the cloud	divine help/new offer.

Theme: The card is depicting a young man not satisfied with the gifts available to him. He is so much focussed on the cups he can't have that he is missing to look what the divine is offering to him.

Keywords : discontentment, looking at others' gift and not oneself.

Zodiac sign	Scorpio.
Nakshatra	Jyestha.
Tarot meaning Overall	discontented, not appreciating what is being offered, not recognising one's own gifts, lack mentality and themes of negative or discord.

Five of Cups

Symbols	**Possibilities/ Significance**
Three cups fallen and two are standing upright	few things are left and a lot has lost/lost 60% and remaining 40%.
Two cups show red colour	blood/death/wine.
One cup showing green colour	Scheel's green or cupric green (arsenic)/poison/ arsenic has its roots in ancient Egypt as well.
Water flowing	river/lake.

Man dressed in black coat till feet with head down and looking at the cups on left.	regret/worried/thinking about the loss/jewish clothing at funeral in ancient history.

Theme: The card is a depiction of loss of lives of Israelites due to poison(snake bites) when they opposed the leadership of Moses as well as the lord. A huge number of Israelites died due to snake bites. Moses asked God to help for which he received the answer to use his staff(bronze serpent) to cure the Israelites.

People lost faith in leadership of Moses and God. Lack of devotion. Only Moses devotion helped to save Israelites.

Zodiac sign	Scorpio.
Nakshatra	Anuradha.
Tarot meaning	consequences of not having devotion or faith, lack of devotion, regrets, huge loss

Overall negative or discord.

Six of Cups

Symbols	**Possibilities/ Significance**
Two houses in the background	residence
A man walking with a javelin or weapon	a guard on duty.
Six cups are there. Four at the bottom, one on the pillar and one being offered	number six significance.
A girl wearing red shoes	child of noble family/ power/aristocrat family/ daughter of a priest.

Female child is wearing gloves in her hand	cold/winter season.
Another child taller than the female offering one cup to her	elder sibling/elder sister/ elder brother.
A mosaic having a cross printed on the pillar	shield of army/militia.
Six white flowers one in each cup	a vine flower that grows in winter/white jasmine/ white jasmine signifies purity and love.

Theme: The card is a depiction of Nashon (the military commander appointed by Moses during Exodus) and his sister Elisheba. Elisheba married Aaron(elder brother of Moses). Nashon and Elisheba were both of noble birth (represented by the white jasmine). She was the high priestess from the tribe of Judah(reference to red shoes in above image). The six cups denotes the six attributes of different leaders of Hebrew. Nashon's ancestor were six men of different qualities David, Messiah, Daniel, Hananiah, Azariah and Mishael(all represented by the cups in the above image).

It talks about the love and purity between two siblings.

Zodiac sign	Pisces.
Nakshatra	Revati.
Tarot meaning	memories of childhood, love and purity, noble or high birth and themes of Revati
Overall	positive or affirmative.

Seven of Cups

<u>**Symbols**</u>	<u>**Possibilities/ Significance**</u>
Seven cups in the cloud	dream/vision.
Face of woman in one cup	prominent person/ Miriam.
Yellow serpent in one cup	staff of Moses/bronze serpent.
A castle in one cup	power/strength/high palace/authority.
Gems and jewels in one cup	riches/prosperity.

A dragon in one cup	reference to Tanin(book of Exodus)/ sea dragon/ Aaron's staff becomes Tanin.
A wreath of olive leaves in one cup	symbol for winner in ancient Egypt/peace and harmony/used in wedding.
A white ghost like figure in one cup	ghost/prophecy/God or angel without a face.
Man's shadow is visible with right hand in shock	shock/fear/anxiety.

Theme: The card is a depiction of dream/vision of Pharaoh during Exodus. He was scared of the prophecy that the Israelites will rebel and overthrow him and thus free themselves of slavery. Due to this vision, Pharaoh ordered to kill all the male child of Israelites to fail the prophecy. However, by then Moses was already conceived and three months old in the womb of her mother Jochebed.

Zodiac sign Scorpio.

Nakshatra	Vishaka pada 4
Tarot meaning	
Overall	difficult choices, visions, dreams, trying to change destiny(or something) that can't be changed, cruelty out of paranoia and negative or discord.

Eight of Cups

Symbols	Possibilities/ Significance
Total eight cups five on the bottom and three on top	family/close members/ group of eight.
Man wearing red robe and red shoes and a staff	high priest/royal person/ prophet.
Two green lush mountains not much above sea level	mountain could be mount Nebo.
Sun and Moon in the sky with closed eyes	more of a compassion/ calm and composed eyes/ neither happy nor sad.

Theme: The card is a depiction of death of Moses. He is ascending the mount Nebo. Moses was asked by God to climb the mountain. The eight cups are reference to Moses' wife, Aaron, Elisheba, Miriam, Nashon, two sons of Moses and Joshua. A prophet who did his part and left behind his legacy " the ten commandments of Moses".

Zodiac sign	Pisces.
Nakshatra	Revati.
Tarot meaning	Leaving legacy behind, final rest to the soul, completion of a meaningful journey
Overall	neutral.

Nine of Cups

Symbols	**Possibilities/ Significance**
Nine cups placed on a higher shelf	attainment of prosperity/ abundance/enjoyment.
Man sitting on bench looking straight, happy face and a red cap on head, crossed hands	young prophet.

Theme: The card is a depiction of Joshua. He was chosen by Moses to lead the Israelites after him. Moses had two sons but instead of choosing them as successor he approved Joshua to lead. Joshua was one of the spies sent to Canaan. He led the Israelites tribe in the conquest of Canaan later on.

Keyword: Choosing an able leader instead of nepotism, one who is worthy.

Zodiac sign	Scorpio.
Nakshatra	Jyestha.
Tarot	having plenty still desires for more, Moon
meaning	in Jyestha, power hungry, proud, over
Overall	positive or affirmative.

Ten of Cups

<u>**Symbols**</u>	<u>**Possibilities/ Significance**</u>
Rainbow in the sky	beauty/peace/colourful season.
Ten cups in the sky	ten commandments of Moses.
A woman and a man looking upward in the sky	reference to fulfilment or joy by following the ten commandments.
Two kids playing	children of the couple/ any kid.

Theme: The card is a depiction of peaceful and happy life by following the ten commandments of Moses.

Zodiac sign	Cancer.
Nakshatra	Pushya.
Tarot meaning	compassion, following rules and regulations, hope, bringing family
Overall	positive or affirmative.

The most strongest bonds are made during the most fragile moments.

Suit of Swords

King of Swords

Symbols	Possibilities/ Significance
Butterfly in the background	re-birth/transformation/ resurrection/connection to Christianity.
Sword	for cutting through things/ weapon.
Man facing forward	determined.

Sitting on a rock in the background	reference to open area.

Theme: The card is a depiction of legendary king Arthur Pendragon with his sword Excalibur.

Zodiac sign	Aquarius.
Nakshatra	Purva Bhadrapada.
Tarot meaning	cutting illusion, involvement with sorcerer, extremely powerful opponent
Overall	positive or affirmative.

Queen of Swords

<u>**Symbols**</u>	<u>**Possibilities/ Significance**</u>
Woman with a crown	queen/royal birth.
Red bracelet on left wrist	a bracelet on left wrist(as in Kabbalah) to ward off misfortune and protect from evil eye. It originated with Rachel in jewish culture and later on adopted in Christianity.
Yellow butterfly on crown	significance of the soul/ hope and guidance.

A picture of a child on the side face of the chair and legs of chair that of a peacock	peacock shows eternity and life after death/child could represent the kid that died/woman who lost a baby or miscarriage.

Theme: The card is a depiction of legendary queen Guinevere (wife of king Arthur Pendragon). Guinevere got herself in love triangle with Lancelot and king Arthur.

Keywords: famous, miscarriage, love triangle.

Zodiac sign	Aquarius.
Nakshatra	Dhanistha.
Tarot meaning	miscarriage, famous, chivalric themes, genesis for war, strong, dancing to one's own music and themes of Dhanistha
Overall	neutral.

Knight of Swords

Symbols	Possibilities/ Significance
Knight	warrior/knighthood.
Wind blowing, trees bending towards right, birds in the sky towards right top	going against the wind/ into the hurricane/ a difficult or dangerous situation.
Horse has skeptical eyes and teeth prominent	horse is scared of the fearlessness of the knight/ horse thinks the rider is crazy.

A small heart symbol on the bridle of horse(crown piece)	love/fight for love or compassion.
Red cardinal bird on breast collar as well as yellow butterflies	red bird is for hope in situation of despair and yellow butterfly representing Guinevere.

Theme: The card is a depiction of famous knight of Arthur's round table, Sir Lancelot. Lancelot rescued Guinevere (wife of king Arthur). He was a friend of king Arthur. The most trusted knight as well as capable one. King Arthur got the Excalibur sword because of the prophecy as he was meant to rule Britons. But it was Lancelot who made the battles victorious along with other knights of the round table.

The only fault of Lancelot was to fall in love with his queen Guinevere and wife of his best friend(King Arthur). It led to the infamous love triangle which was the genesis for the fall of entire round table(knights of round table) of King Arthur.

Zodiac sign	Libra.
Nakshatra	Vishakha.
Tarot meaning	fighting for love, warrior, moving towards goal with force, betrayal in friendship, fixated, moving into dangerous situations
Overall	positive or affirmative.

Page of Swords

Symbols	Possibilities/ Significance
A young man with red shoes holding a sword	prominent person because of red shoes/high born.
Wind blowing hair in opposite direction	dramatic effect given by the creator/ wind is not so strong as the cloud and birds position remain unaffected.
Standing on a rock	elevation/significance with rock or elevation.
Sword	Excalibur.

Theme: The card is a depiction of young Arthur Pendragon (son of Uther Pendragon) later to be known as king Arthur. Arthur is drawing the famous sword Excalibur from the stone after hearing a prophecy from Merlin. The prophecy was ; whoever is capable to draw out the sword will rule the Britons. Arthur drew the sword at a very young age that's why the above image is representing the left hand as inappropriately holding the sword. Arthur succeeded in two attempts. In first attempt he loosen up the sword and he pulled it out in the second attempt.

Zodiac sign	Gemini.
Nakshatra	Punarvasu.
Tarot meaning	rag to riches, aligned with one's destiny, need two attempts for success, taking one's rightful place and themes of

Overall   positive or affirmative.

Ace of Swords

Theme: The card is a depiction of the prophecy which Merlin narrated. Any man who pulls out the Excalibur sword will rule the Britons. It was not clear whether the prophecy was created and carefully crafted by Merlin himself. Merlin was a sorcerer. Arthur Pendragon son of Uther Pendragon was the one who pulled the sword and became the king.

Zodiac sign   Gemini.

Nakshatra	Mrigasira.
Tarot meaning Overall	prophecy, vision, an idea or pursuit that will become trendsetter, hope, revival, magic, innovation and themes of positive or affirmative.

Two of Swords

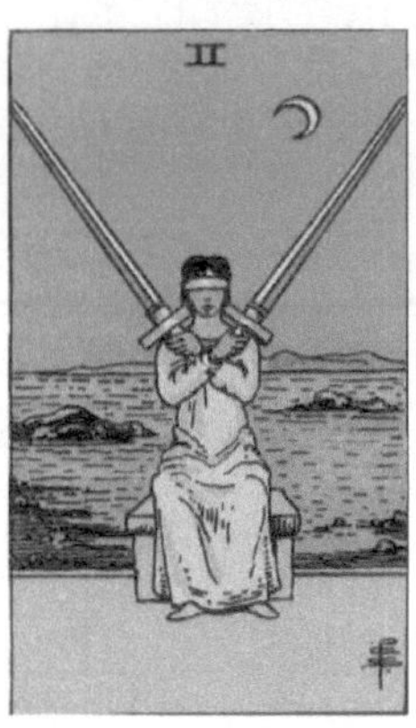

Symbols	**Possibilities/ Significance**
A woman blindfolded	can't see/unbiased judgement.
Two swords in different direction	two choices/dilemma about two things.
a crescent moon in the sky	fertility/menstruating women/someone who is not a mother yet.

Theme: The card is a depiction of queen Guinevere trouble in making choices between king Arthur and Sir Lancelot. All three became part of the love triangle.

Zodiac sign	Libra.
Nakshatra	Vishakha.
Tarot meaning	two different choices, dilemma, trouble position, difficult situations, two potential mates or ideas and themes of Vishakha
Overall	negative or discord.

Three of Swords

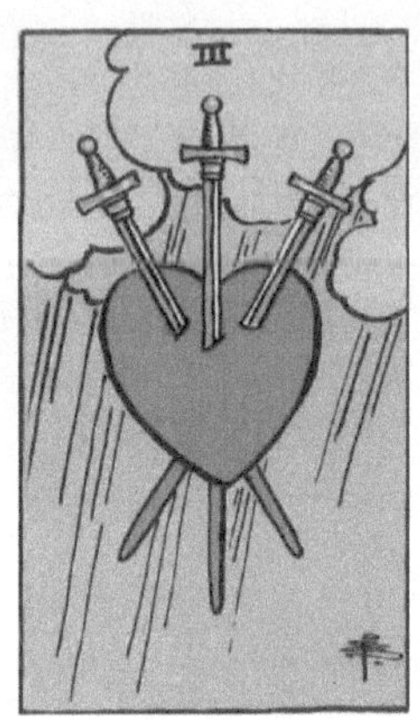

Theme: The card is a depiction of love triangle of Arthur, Guinevere and Lancelot. The chivalric romance that become famous widely.

Zodiac sign	Aquarius.
Nakshatra	Dhanistha.
Tarot meaning	Third party situation, three is a crowd, love triangle, Moon in Dhanistha nakshatra pada 3, 7th lord in Dhanistha
Overall	negative or discord.

Four of Swords

Theme: The card is a depiction of a knight praying the night before battle. It was a practice among knights to sleep in their coffin prior to battle because they don't know whether they will return alive or not. Therefore they pray and be grateful for the nights they had.

Zodiac sign	Libra.
Nakshatra	Swati.
Tarot meaning	peace, deep rest, patience, gratitude for everything and themes of Swati

Overall neutral.

Five of Swords

Symbols	**Possibilities/ Significance**
Two people in background, one person crying	disappointment/grief/ loss/left their sword as if they lost the battle or hope.
A man picking up swords with grinning face	cunning/smart ass/ someone who outmanoeuvred others.

Theme: The card is a depiction of Modred (another knight of round table) who convinced everyone that king Arthur is dead and usurped the throne for himself. It lead to the battle of Camlann later on. The card shows spreading misinformation or rumours to achieve one's motive.

Keywords: sneaky, misinformation, rumour, knight, usurper, crying.

Zodiac sign	Gemini.
Nakshatra	Ardra.
Tarot	cunning, misinformation, sneaky,
meaning	notional loss, theft, loss of articles and
Overall	negative or discord.

Six of Swords

Symbols	**Possibilities/**
Six swords	trouble/obstacles.
A small child and another person covered	leaving place of difficulties.
A boatman/ferryman	travelling/taking

Theme: The card is a depiction of child Arthur being taken away by Merlin to raise in a foster home under the care of Ector. Because of the prophecy that the child of

Uther Pendragon will become the ruler of England, the Saxons wanted to eliminate the threat. Uther asked Merlin to guide Arthur and raise him in secret till the time he becomes ready to rule.

Keywords: secret, foster home, leaving trouble waters.

Zodiac sign	Aquarius.
Nakshatra	Satabhisaj.
Tarot meaning	Secrecy for the greater good, moving away from troubled waters, voyage, long distance travel, support from unknown
Overall	neutral.

Seven of Swords

Symbols	**Possibilities/ Significance**
Tents in background	military camp.
A boat in the background with men onboard	invasion/war between two armies.
Man carrying five swords only and two remaining	stealing vital information/ stealing informations/ attack with a surprise/ cunning.
Man wearing red shoes and a red cap	sorcerer/prominent personality.

Theme: The card is a depiction of cunning magician Merlin. He is aiding Arthur Pendragon in the battle against saxons. Initially he helped Uther Pendragon and later his son Arthur. Merlin always had a habit of meddling with magic. The trickster of the Arthurian legend.

Zodiac sign	Libra.
Nakshatra	Chitra.
Tarot meaning	trickster, magician, stealing vital information, striking where it hurts most,
Overall	neutral.

Eight of Swords

Symbols	**Possibilities/ Significance**
A castle on top of hill	prominent castle/Tintagel castle.
Eight swords around the woman but not obstructing path	defence barricade/security perimeter.
Woman is blindfolded and hands tied behind back	couldn't see nor could take any action.

Theme: The card is a depiction of birthplace(place of conception) of king Arthur; “Tintagel castle”. The woman in the picture is Igraine(mother of king Arthur). Igraine was the wife of Goloris (a warlord during times of Uther Pendragon) and later became the wife of Uther Pendragon. Uther Pendragon was enchanted by her beauty so much that he lusted for her. Uther took the help of Merlin’s magic to achieve this lecherous motive. Uther disguised as Goloris slept with Igraine and thus the conception of Arthur happened. Igraine couldn’t identify her husband because of the magic(reference to the blindfold in the above image). Goloris died in the battle same night. Goloris had put Igraine in Tintagel castle under his security before leaving for the battle.

Zodiac sign	Libra.
Nakshatra	Chitra pada 4
Tarot meaning	mala fide use of magic, deception, feeling powerless, scheming, deceiving contracts, making one sign on the dotted line,

Overall negative or discord.

Nine of Swords

Symbols	Possibilities/ Significance
Nine swords in the background	knights of round table.
Man waking up and face covered	grief/despair/crying.
Left bottom has image of two persons fighting with sword	Battle of Camlann; Modred and Arthur killing each other.

Theme: The card is a depiction of Sir Lancelot after the demise of king Arthur. He was in grief. Although he had differences with king Arthur because of falling in love with Guinevere. Lancelot was Arthur's best friend. Lancelot gave up his armour and exchanged it for clothes of a monk.

Zodiac sign	Gemini.
Nakshatra	Ardra.
Tarot meaning	grief, regret, loss, death of loved ones, weeping, insomnia, disturbed sleep
Overall	negative or discord.

Ten of Swords

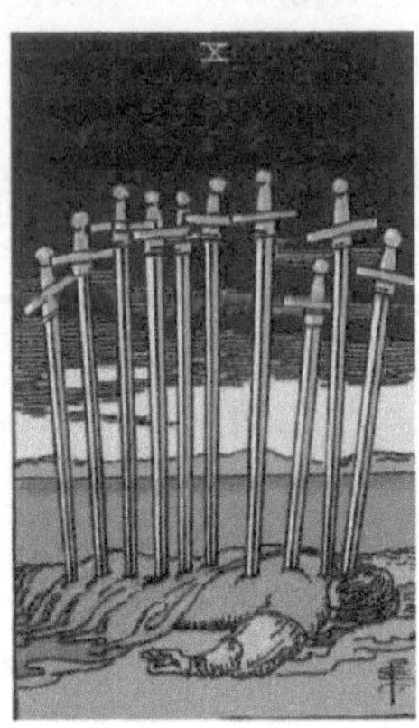

Symbols	**Possibilities/ Significance**
Ten swords in back	betrayal/ people closest betrayed/usurping.
Man dead with blood on the floor also covered with red cloth	prominent person is dead/ a king died or killed/ a powerful person who was killed.
The hand showing letter 'U' in ASL(sign language)	reference to king Uther Pendragon.

Theme: The card is a depiction of death/assassination of king Uther (father of Arthur Pendragon) by his own daughter Morgana Pendragon(Arthur's half sister).

Keywords: assassination, trouble between father and his girl child, coup.

Zodiac sign	Gemini.
Nakshatra	Ardra.
Tarot meaning	assassination, trouble between father and girl child, a coup, attempt on life, failure of project or business due to moles within
Overall	negative or discord.

At any point in time a person is exactly where he is supposed to be or he will reach exactly where is meant to be.

Suit of Pentacles

King of Pentacles

Symbols	Possibilities/ Significance
Grapes on the clothes	vineyard.
A scepter	king/royal person.
Castle in background	kingdom/authority.
Bull on four corners of chair	Taurus zodiac/stubborn/ bull headed.

Sabaton shoes	knight/warrior.
Shoe placed on a stone	stone having eyes as if someone's head/head of an animal.
Person's face is looking downwards at the pentacle	smirking face/cunning/ proud about achievement of the pentacle.
Red keffiyeh draped around the neck	connection with Jewish or Palestine.

Theme: The card is a depiction of story of king Ahab and Naboth's vineyard. Ahab was the seventh king of Israel, the son and successor of king Omri. He was the husband of Jezebel of Sidon.

Ahab desired to acquire Naboth's vineyard so that he could use it for a vegetable or a herb garden. When Ahab returned to his palace sad because Naboth refused to sell his vineyard as per mosaic law, his wife Jezebel instigated him. She falsely accused Naboth of treachery and got him stoned to death.

Love of a queen for her king (and husband) made her commit a great crime. It was an extreme greediness to the point of taking someone's life.

Ahab and Jezebel both were warned by prophet Elijah for this crime. Ahab also had a lot of encounters with prophets.

Keyword: vineyard, bull headed, attracted to other person's abundance, influenced by wife or partner.

Zodiac sign	Taurus.
Nakshatra	Rohini.
Tarot meaning	being bull headed to achieve the goals by any means, jealous, fall because of one's own partner (husband/wife), one who likes gardening, into agriculture business, bad advice, achieving monetary abundance at the expense of others,
Overall	neutral.

Queen of Pentacles

Symbols	Possibilities/ Significance
Women with a crown	royal/queen.
Goat on the corner of chair	Capricorn zodiac.
holding a pentacle	abundance.
Child on the top of the chair	mother/expecting to be a mother.
Hare or rabbit at the right bottom	In Bible, Hare are denoted as unclean animal therefore portrayed in a negative way.

Red colour of hare	hunting of hare/hunting/ blood.

Theme: The card is a depiction of Athaliah (queen of Judah). Athaliah was daughter of Ahab and Jezebel. She was married to Jehoram (king of Judah). After the death of her son Ahaziah she seized the throne of Judah and ordered execution of all the claimants to the throne. She was termed as "usurper queen".

Mother grieved by the loss of her child and became extremely cruel. She seized the opportunity as soon as it arrived.

Zodiac sign	Virgo.
Nakshatra	Chitra.
Tarot meaning	usurper, taking by force, seizing opportunity, loss of children, separation from child, devoted mother and themes
Overall	neutral.

Knight of Pentacles

Symbols	**Possibilities/ Significance**
Black horse	fourth horse of apocalypse/famine/ judgement.
Armour and saddle has red colour	blood/death/bloodshed/ slaughter.
Hanging coat from the saddle	reference to someone's coat/someone who was killed and laded on a horse.

Club moss like plant on knight's helmet and horse head	club moss is also known as wolf's claw. Just like a wolf hunt its prey, the creator used it as an allegory to denote the ferocious and cunning ways of someone.

Theme: The card is a depiction of Jehu (son of Jehoshaphat) and king of northern kingdom of Israel. He was responsible for the divine judgement against the house of Ahab(as believed in history). He literally slaughtered many. He killed king Jehoram(son of Ahab) and threw his body on Naboth's vineyard (refer to the coat on the saddle in the above image). During his reign he executed many people and was invincible as well as cruel.

Zodiac sign	Capricorn.
Nakshatra	Uttara Asadha.
Tarot meaning	invincible, ruthless, execution, dangerous opponent, judgement, tit for tat and
Overall	neutral.

Page of Pentacles

Symbols	**Possibilities/ Significance**
Red cap/turban	prophet/priest.
Young man offering pentacle with both hands	apprentice.

Theme: The card is a depiction of apprentice Elisha(later became prophet). Elisha was a disciple and protege of Elijah. It was during the reign of king Ahab.

Zodiac sign	Virgo.
Nakshatra	Hasta.
Tarot meaning	apprentice, prophet, magician, protege, studious, excellent academic records, financial managers, accountants and
Overall	positive or affirmative.

Ace of Pentacles

Theme: The card is depiction of new beginnings and abundance. In the background there are white lilies which symbolises purity. The archway is a reference to the vineyard of Naboth which was given to him by his ancestors. It was the genesis of cascading events that led to the fall of house of king Ahab of Judah.

Zodiac sign Taurus.

Nakshatra	Rohini.
Tarot	material abundance, food and
meaning	agriculture, legacy, heritage and themes
Overall	positive or affirmative.

Two of Pentacles

<u>**Symbols**</u>	<u>**Possibilities/ Significance**</u>
Two ships in turbulent water	turbulence/problem.
a person with red hat	prominent person/person with power.
Balancing two coins	juggling between two different things/ working two things simultaneously.
Infinity symbol	endless/limitless.

Theme: The card is a depiction of Ahaziah of Israel (son of Ahab) forming a business partnership with king of Judah to have a fleet of trading ships. However, the ships were wrecked and never set sail.

Zodiac sign	Virgo.
Nakshatra	Hasta.
Tarot meaning	incorrect aspirations, failure even after multiple attempts, Jupiter in Hasta and
Overall	negative or discord.

Three of Pentacles

<u>**Symbols**</u>	<u>**Possibilities/ Significance**</u>
Three pentacles on a pillar	reference to three people/ crowd.
a man standing on a bench holding a mallet in his right hand and a chisel in left hand	worker/craftsman.
Two person standing near and showing a map	a design/architectural design/map/to build something.
Woman has red colour on her clothes	prominent person.

Man in black attire	priest/escorting the other person.

Theme: The card is a depiction of queen Jezebel of Sidon (wife of king Ahab of Israel) asking the craftsman to build a pillar for her worship of Ba'al religion which was different than Yahweh(of Israel).

Zodiac sign	Virgo.
Nakshatra	Chitra.
Tarot meaning	Something new to be created, seeking professional help, creation of something
Overall	neutral.

Four of Pentacles

Symbols	**Possibilities/ Significance**
Crown	king/prince.
One pentacle on head, one holding close to chest and two pentacles below feet	abundant king/blessed with wealth and following in father's footstep.

Theme: The card is a depiction of Ahaziah of Israel(son of king Ahab) who followed in his father's footsteps of worshipping a different religion Ba'al.

Keywords: like father like son, ancestral wealth, fruit of the same tree.

Zodiac sign	Virgo.
Nakshatra	Uttara Phalguni.
Tarot meaning	Walking in father's footsteps, ancestral wealth, born with golden spoon in mouth
Overall	neutral.

Five of Pentacles

Symbols	**Possibilities/ Significance**
glass window with five pentacles	abundance/prosperity.
a man on elbow crutches and small in height	challenged by disability.
a woman walking past the window out in the cold	blind woman/can't see the lights and the warmth behind the glass.

Theme: The card is a depiction of two differently abled person. One can't walk properly and another can't see.

Therefore both can't see what is in front of them. Only if both combined their skills together the scenario would have been completely different. If the lame showed the way and the blind carried him on her shoulder then they would have seen the glass window instead of wandering out in the cold. The card shows two people troubled and engrossed in their own miseries so much that they are unable to see the light of God. Instead of focussing on one's own miseries if they tried to connect with each other and helped each other both of their fates would have been different.

Keywords: combined efforts, need to connect with others, able to see the silver lining.

Zodiac sign Capricorn.
Nakshatra Shravana.

	combined efforts, need to connect with
Tarot meaning	others, able to see the silver lining, listen to other people or your partner, a person who limps, Saturn in Shravana
Overall	negative or discord.

Six of Pentacles

Symbols	**Possibilities/ Significance**
Two person sitting at bottom	beggars/underprivileged people.
Person on the left with open hands but not catching the coins or grains	blind person.
person on the right	connection with person on left/couple/friends/same people from previous card of the Tarot deck.
A man standing and holding a scale in left hand	balance/unbiased/ judgement/merchant.

Man's right hand two fingers are suppressing the coins or grains	not giving whole heartedly/business man / merchant/capitalist.
Six pentacles in the background	number six significance.

Theme: The card is a depiction of Jehoram (king of Judah). He killed six of his brothers. He was the son of king Jehoshaphat. He married Athaliah (daughter of king Ahab of Israel) to strengthen his position. The card tells about businessman, a politically aspiring person as well as crafty.

Zodiac sign	Virgo.
Nakshatra	Chitra.
Tarot meaning Overall	businessman, crafty person, merchant, politically motivated and themes of negative or discord.

Seven of Pentacles

Theme: The card is showing a commoner awaiting for his harvest for all the efforts he has put in. Leaves represents vineyard. It may be a representation of commoner 'Naboth' who had a vineyard which was the genesis for cascading events for the house of Ahab of Israel.

Zodiac sign	Taurus.
Nakshatra	Mrigasira.
Tarot meaning	Slow growth, needs patience and themes of Mrigasira nakshatra.

Overall neutral.

Eight of Pentacles

Theme: The card is a depiction of a craftsman working on the pillar of Ba'al which was stated in three of pentacles card. The craftsman is meticulously making it. Even though the pillar is completed but he is still working.

Keywords: Workaholic, meticulously making something.

Zodiac sign	Capricorn.
Nakshatra	Dhanistha.

Tarot meaning	workaholic, meticulously making something and themes of Dhanistha
Overall	positive or affirmative.

Nine of Pentacles

Symbols	**Possibilities/ Significance**
A woman with red cap	prominent person/ priestess/queen/high born.
Vineyard with nine pentacles	a vineyard that is abundant/prosperity/ abundance.
an eagle with eyes covered and sitting on the left hand of the women(on her gloves)	eagle denotes strength/ petting an eagle denotes strength.

a small snail on the bottom left	In Hebrew, snail is used to denote unclean similar to lizards, dogs/creator may have used to denote canaanites.

Theme: The card is a depiction of queen Jezebel of Sidon (wife of king Ahab of Israel). Jezebel practiced the religion of ba'al instead of Yahweh. She used force and trickery to seize Naboth's vineyard because her husband desired it. She is known as a false prophet(reference to red cap and snail at the bottom in the above image).

She helped her own husband to get his desires fulfilled even going to extreme lengths for it.

Zodiac sign	Virgo.
Nakshatra	Hasta.
Tarot meaning	Getting one's desire in one's hand, going extreme lengths for spouse, unscrupulous ways of making money and themes of
Overall	neutral.

Ten of Pentacles

Symbols	**Possibilities/ Significance**
Two dogs	animals/beast/unclean.
One dog being petted by old man	compassion.
Small child holding tail of the dog	dogs in ancient jewish history were termed as beast, unclean and were kept away from children therefore the child is not jewish/ child from different religion.

Two persons at the archway	one is gatekeeper holding a javelin/entry of a castle/ person in red explaining something.
a symbol of castle on a mosaic on top left of archway	symbol for tribe of Simon.
a symbol of scale below the mosaic	tribe of Dan/justice/ merchant.
Three red flags on first mosaic	number three/third son/ three person.
Two red flags just above scale	number two/second son/ two person.
an image of a person in extreme top left	a woman screaming.
a castle below the image of the person	castle denotes strength/ palace/authority/abode.
old man with white hair having image of grapes on clothes	abundance/wine/ celebration.

Theme: The card is a depiction of joining forces of Simon (third son of Jacob) and Levi (second son of Jacob) to avenge the rape of their sister Dinah by a Canaanite. Simon and Levi killed all the men of

Shechem and plundered everything including their wives and children.

The card shows the love of brothers towards their sister to avenge her and give justice yet mercilessly slaughtering so many men just for the sins of few which is again ruthless.

Zodiac sign	Capricorn.
Nakshatra	Dhanistha.
Tarot meaning	love for sibling, ruthless, conquering, abundance with emptiness, paternity
Overall	neutral.

बिन माँगे मोती मिलें और माँगे मिले न भीक

Suit of Wands

King of Wands

Symbols	**Possibilities/ Significance**
Only king in entire minor arcana whose eyes can't be seen due to side facing	arrogance/disinterested/ disgust.

The chair has symbol of lion	symbol for tribe of Judah/ initially lion symbol was associated with kingdom of Judah and later on became the symbol for tribe of Judah.
a lizard on the bottom right	lizard are also considered unclean as per Bible/ creator uses it to denote Canaanites or Ammonites.
a lizard chasing its own tail	defensive position of lizard/the man in the image is a descendant of Canaanite or Ammonite or a cross over.

Theme: The card is a depiction of Rehoboam (king of kingdom of Judah). He was the son of Solomon and Naamah. Solomon was son of David and Naamah was an ammonite. History depicts Rehoboam as an arrogant king. His arrogance could be due to the fact that he was the son of wise judge Solomon. He didn't have to work hard and all was given to him by his paternal lineage.

Zodiac sign	Leo.
Nakshatra	Magha.
Tarot meaning	ancestral wealth or privileges, arrogant, forceful and themes of Magha nakshatra.
Overall	negative or discord.

Queen of Wands

Symbols	**Possibilities/ Significance**
a bright woman with a crown	queen/beautiful queen
Two lions holding sunflower in the background	symbol for tribe of Judah/ Bastet symbol/connection to Egypt.
Sunflower in left hand	sunflower always looks at the sun (could be an indirect reference to wife of son)/sunflower seeds being used in wicca or magic in ancient Egypt.

a black cat sitting at the bottom	reference to witches/bad omen in jewish history/ worshipped in Egypt as Goddess Bastet. Bastet initial symbol was a form of lioness and later a cat. She was protector of children, associated with female fertility and sexuality.
left feet of the woman is in red colour	high born/daughter of a priest.

Theme: The card is a depiction of Tamar who was the daughter-in-law of Judah (son of Jacob) and later became the mother of his twin sons Perez and Zerah.

Tamar's husband Er (eldest son of Judah) died after which Judah asked his second son Onan to enter into levirate marriage with Tamar. Onan was asked to procreate with Tamar to continue the lineage but he died as well. Judah had three sons Er, Onan and Shelah. When two of his sons died he thought Tamar is cursed and he refused to let his youngest son Shelah into levirate marriage with his brother's widow.

Tamar wanted to secure her place in the royal lineage of tribe of Judah. She outsmarted Judah(father-in-law) by disguising herself as a prostitute and got herself pregnant. She bore twin sons.

Keywords: Aspiration to become mother, magic, beautiful, scandalous relationship, incest, passionate

Zodiac sign	Leo.
Nakshatra	Purva Phalguni.
Tarot meaning	aspiration to become mother, magic, beautiful, scandalous relationship, incest, passionate, Mars in Purva Phalguni and
Overall	negative or discord.

Knight of Wands

Theme: The card is a depiction of invasion of Judah by Egypt. The pharaoh's army invaded Judah and plundered all the riches from the temple of Judah. The treaty between Egypt and Israel ended with death of Solomon. Solomon did many political marriages, one of which was marrying Naamah(princess of Ammon). He signed a treaty of peace among the two kingdoms.

Zodiac sign	Sagittarius.
Nakshatra	Purva Asadha.
Tarot meaning	breaking treaties, preparing for battle, invasion of privacy and themes of Purva
Overall	neutral.

Page of Wands

Theme: Three pyramids in the background shows Egypt connection. A man holding a wand and donning a hat with a feather on top of it. The feather on cap is a depiction of achievement. The card is a depiction of Pharaoh of Egypt during invasion of kingdom of Judah. The Pharaoh's army ransacked Jerusalem. He was able to unify Libyans, Sukkits and Ethiopians together to invade Judah(reference to the feather on the cap).

Zodiac sign   Sagittarius.

Nakshatra	Mula.
Tarot	destroying religious places, radicals,
meaning	plundering, iconoclast, unearned wealth,
Overall	neutral.

Ace of Wands

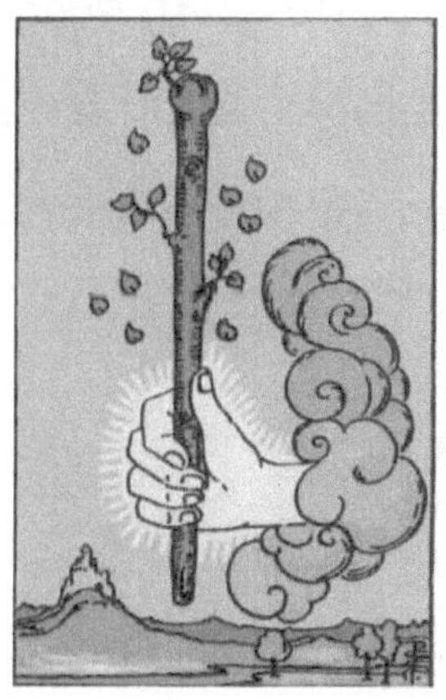

Theme: A castle in the background with a tower in it. A cloud holding a wand(phallic) with total eighteen leaves around it. The castle and the tower are reference to tower of David. And the eighteen leaves signify children of David (king of Israel).

The card is a depiction of lineage of house of David. It is the house from which major events happened that reshaped the entire jewish history.

Zodiac sign   Aries.

Nakshatra	Bharani.
Tarot meaning	procreation, marriage, virile, passionate beginnings, child birth, Sun in Bharani
Overall	positive or affirmative.

Two of Wands

Symbols	**Possibilities/ Significance**
Two wands	balance.
Two flowers; lilies and roses	peace as well as power.
man holding a globe	king/emperor/authority figure.
Globe has red colour in distant areas not adjacent	domination in distant areas/allies/vassal.
man wearing red hat/ crown	prophet/king/priest.

Theme: The card is a depiction of king Solomon holding the globe and forging alliance with different religion(or geographies). He was an example of wisdom as well as power.

Zodiac sign	Taurus.
Nakshatra	Rohini.
Tarot meaning	forging alliances, equilibrium, power and wisdom in one, business leaders, global business and themes of Rohini nakshatra.
Overall	positive or affirmative.

Three of Wands

Theme: A man wearing a crown and armour of a knight. There are three wands around him and looking at the ships. He is also wearing red shoes.

The card could be a depiction of a scout looking at the upcoming ships or king Abijah of Judah himself on the mount of Zemaraim looking at the dead sea or its tributaries. He is preparing for the upcoming battle.

Zodiac sign	Sagittarius.
Nakshatra	Purva Asadha.

Tarot meaning	scouting, looking from above, planning, beginning of battle and themes of Purva
Overall	positive or affirmative.

Four of Wands

Symbols	Possibilities/ Significance
a chuppah	a canopy used in jewish wedding.
only two wands are tied and rest two wands are not	may be wands in pair/2 & 2/ 11 & 11/22 number.
a castle in the background and people rejoicing	marriage ceremony/ celebration.

Theme: It is a depiction of marriage in Jewish tradition. Since the whole suit of wands mostly talk about Abijah of Judah. Therefore the number 22 in above card could be a reference to his 22 sons. The card is all about marriage and celebration.

Zodiac sign	Leo.
Nakshatra	Uttara Phalguni.
Tarot	marriage, wealth through marriage,
meaning	prosperity, celebration and themes of
Overall	positive or affirmative.

Five of Wands

Theme: Five person are cheering with their respective wands. A prowess is depicted in the card. It could be an indication of the handpicked men of Abijah's army.

Zodiac sign	Sagittarius.
Nakshatra	Uttara Asadha.
Tarot meaning	competition, proving one's worth, combat trials and themes of Uttara
Overall	neutral.

Six of Wands

Theme: The card is a depiction of coronation of king Abijah of Judah(son of Rehoboam) and grandson of Solomon. He became a king at a very young age(around eighteen years).

Zodiac sign	Leo.
Nakshatra	Uttara Phalguni.
Tarot meaning	coronation of kings and queens, royal favours, favours from government, recognition, victorious and themes of
Overall	positive or affirmative.

Seven of Wands

Theme: The card is a depiction of battle of mount Zemaraim between Abijah of Judah and Jeroboam of Israel. Abijah's army were handpicked men plus they had the vantage point. They crushed 500,000 of Israelites in the battle and rest of the Israelites fled away.

Zodiac sign	Sagittarius.
Nakshatra	Mula.
Tarot meaning	crushing opponents, defeating all, battleground, vantage point and Mula
Overall	positive or affirmative.

Eight of Wands

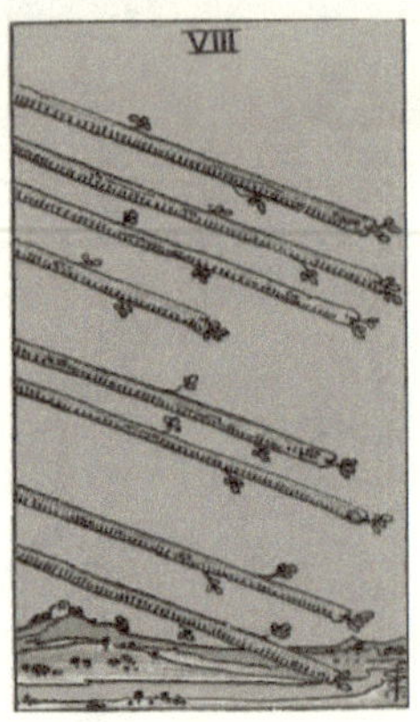

Theme: It is a depiction of attack from behind by Jeroboam's army towards Abijah's army at mount Zemaraim. Abijah had 400,000 handpicked men and Jeroboam had 800,000 warriors and still Jeroboam couldn't defeat Abijah. Jeroboam executed a pincer movement towards Abijah's army but Abijah's men counter attacked very well and eliminated 500,000 of Jeroboam's men.

Zodiac sign Aries.

Nakshatra	Krittika.
Tarot meaning	countering hidden motives, militant intelligence, strong survival instincts, ambush, hidden surprises, attack from
Overall	neutral.

Nine of Wands

Theme: This card is a depiction of the battle won at mount Zemaraim. Abijah's army crushed Jeroboam and still standing.

Zodiac sign	Sagittarius.
Nakshatra	Purva Asadha.
Tarot	invincible, last man standing, victorious,
meaning	fighting for a cause and themes of Purva
Overall	positive or affirmative.

Ten of Wands

Theme: The card is a depiction of Abijah of Judah (son of Rehoboam) trying to bring back the ten tribes of northern Israel to their allegiance. The path which his father Rehoboam refused to follow. Abijah's attempt to unify the tribes continued throughout his lifetime but he failed in his endeavour.

Zodiac sign	Sagittarius.
Nakshatra	Purva Asadha.
Tarot meaning	completion of task even if it's failure, end of projects, winding up and themes of

Overall negative or discord.

When compassion is taken as weakness music is bound to follow, which will be either of the divine or that of a judge.

References

1. https://en.wikipedia.org/wiki/Moses

2. https://en.wikipedia.org/wiki/Joseph_(Genesis)

3. https://en.wikipedia.org/wiki/King_Arthur

4. https://en.wikipedia.org/wiki/Guinevere

5. https://en.wikipedia.org/wiki/Lancelot

6. https://en.wikipedia.org/wiki/Battle_of_Camlann

7. https://en.wikipedia.org/wiki/Tamar_(Genesis)

8. https://en.wikipedia.org/wiki/Abijah_of_Judah

9. https://en.wikipedia.org/wiki/Jochebed

10. https://en.wikipedia.org/wiki/Ahab

11. https://en.wikipedia.org/wiki/Jezebel

12. https://en.wikipedia.org/wiki/Athaliah

13. https://en.wikipedia.org/wiki/David

14. https://en.wikipedia.org/wiki/Dinah

15. https://en.wikipedia.org/wiki/Nahshon

www.ingramcontent.com/pod-product-compliance
Lightning Source LLC
LaVergne TN
LVHW041102150826
845673LV00007B/1890
9798892771887